THE BASIC BOOK OF
SCALES, CHORDS,
ARPEGGIOS & CADENCES

Includes all the Major, Minor (Natural, Harmonic, Melodic)
& Chromatic Scales

WILLARD A. PALMER • MORTON MANUS • AMANDA VICK LETHCO

"I don't like to practice, never have. But when I do get started at the piano, for the first 10 minutes I play scales, slowly. I've done this all my life. Listen to the sounds you make. The sound of each tone will generate a response in you. It will give you energy." Van Cliburn

"Do you ask me how good a player you may become? Then tell me how much you practice the scales." Carl Czerny

"I consider the practice of scales important not only for the fingers, but also for the discipline of the ear with regard to the feeling of tonality (key), understanding of intervals, and the comprehension of the total compass of the piano." Josef Hofmann

"Give special study to passing the thumb under the hand and passing the hand over the thumb. This makes the practice of scales and arpeggios indispensable." Jan Paderewski

"Scales should never be dry. If you are not interested in them, work with them until you do become interested in them." Artur Rubinstein

"I believe this matter of insisting upon a thorough technical knowledge, particularly scale playing, is a very vital one. The mere ability to play a few pieces does not constitute musical proficiency." Sergei Rachmaninoff

"You must diligently practice all scales." Robert Schumann

The importance of scales and arpeggios, particularly with regard to the pianist's ability to perform, cannot be overestimated. To trace the development of the major and minor scales through the history of music would require many pages, but we do know that these scales had their origins in the system of modes that was developed in ancient Greek music and music of the Church.

In ancient Greece, certain musical tribes used a lyre, a four-stringed harp called the *tetrachordon* (*tetra* meaning four). The four tones encompassed by this instrument constituted a perfect 4th, and were called a tetrachord. This was the building block that was to become the basis for our modern scales.

On the keyboard, a tetrachord consists of a whole step, a whole step and a half step. If we play a tetrachord beginning on C, we have the notes C, D, E and F. If we begin a second tetrachord on G, we have the notes G, A, B and C. The last C of this tetrachord is exactly one octave higher than the low C of the first tetrachord. These two tetrachords, played in succession, make an eight-note scale in the Ionian mode, which we now know as a major scale. If we use the same tones beginning on the 6th note of the combined two tetrachords, we get the notes A, B, C, D, E, F, G and A. These notes constitute the Aeolian mode, which is also known as our natural minor scale.

The Greek philosopher Pythagorus (around 500 BC) is credited with the discovery of the numerical ratios corresponding to the principal intervals of the musical scale. With an instrument known as a *monochord*, consisting of one string stretched over a long sounding-board, Pythagorus found that by dividing the string into 2 equal parts, one part, when vibrated, would give a tone exactly one octave above the natural tone of the whole string. By sounding 2/3 of the length of the string, the interval of a 5th above the natural tone would be produced. By sounding 3/4 of the length of the string, the interval of a 4th would be produced. In similar manner, the ratios of all the notes of the scale were discovered.

With the ongoing evolution of stringed and keyboard instruments, our modern major and minor scales were developed, and the various temperaments associated with all of the ancient and modern tunings were ultimately derived.

HOW THIS BOOK IS ORGANIZED

Cover design: Martha Widmann/Ted Engelbart
Book production: Bruce Goldes

Part 1

Key of C Major
Major Scales

LH: 4th finger on D (2nd degree of scale).   **RH:** 4th finger on B (7th degree of scale).*

Parallel motion in octaves.

Contrary motion starting on the same note.

Parallel motion in thirds or tenths.

Parallel motion in sixths.

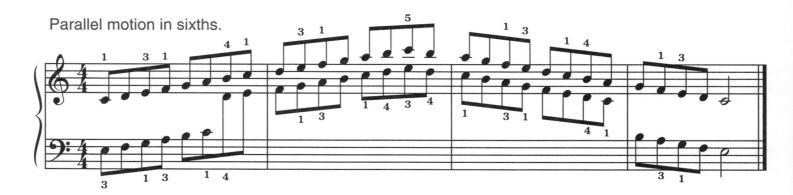

*The 4th finger is usually used only once in an octave. The 4th finger is important because if you know the position of the 4th finger, you can figure out the position of the other fingers. Because of this, the 4th finger of each hand and the degree of the scale it falls on is shown at the top of the scale pages that follow for each major and minor scale. When there is an exception it is so noted just above the music.

C Major Triads Root position

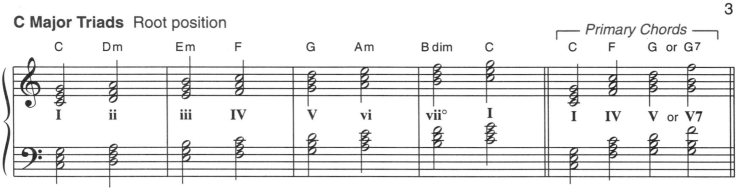

C	Dm	Em	F	G	Am	B dim	C	⌐ Primary Chords ┐
I	ii	iii	IV	V	vi	vii°	I	C F G or G7
								I IV V or V7

tonic   supertonic   mediant   subdominant   dominant   submediant   leading tone   tonic

C Major Cadences Three Positions

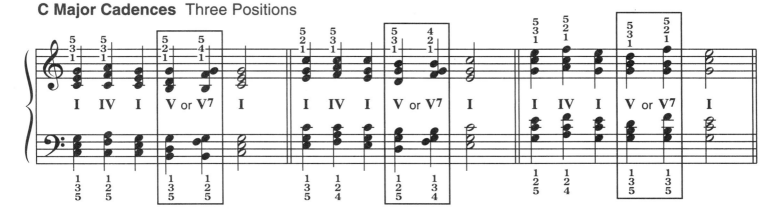

I   IV   I   V or V7   I   I   IV   I   V or V7   I   I   IV   I   V or V7   I

C Major Arpeggios Two-octave arpeggios

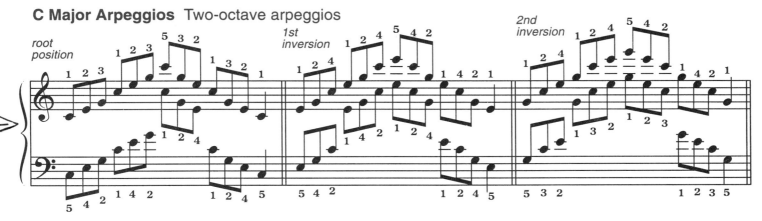

root position   *1st inversion*   *2nd inversion*

Dominant Seventh Arpeggios Two-octave arpeggios

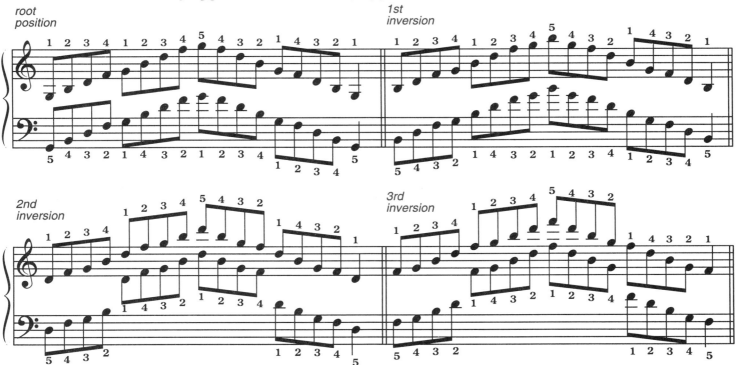

root position   *1st inversion*

2nd inversion   *3rd inversion*

Key of G Major
Major Scales

LH: 4th finger on A (2nd degree). **RH:** 4th finger on F♯ (7th degree).

Parallel motion in octaves.

Contrary motion starting on the same note.

Parallel motion in thirds or tenths.

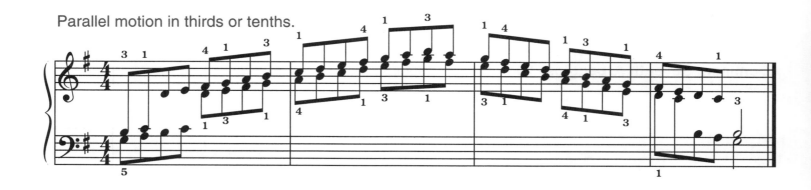

Parallel motion in sixths.

G Major Triads Root position

tonic   supertonic   mediant   subdominant   dominant   submediant   leading tone   tonic

G Major Cadences Three Positions

G Major Arpeggios Two-octave arpeggios

Dominant Seventh Arpeggios Two-octave arpeggios

Key of D Major
Major Scales

LH: 4th finger on E (2nd degree).   **RH:** 4th finger on C# (7th degree).

Parallel motion in octaves.

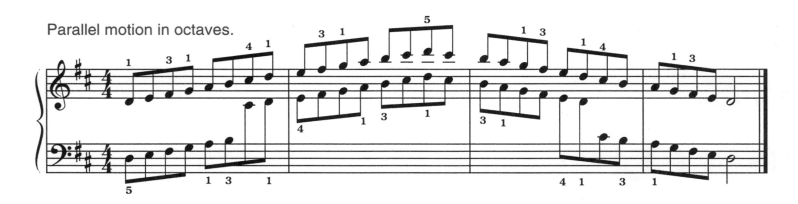

Contrary motion starting on the same note.

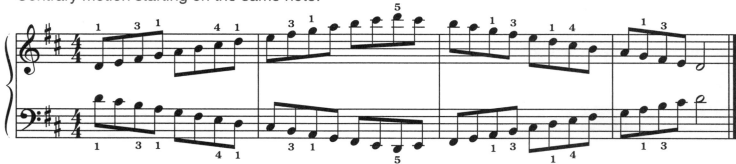

Parallel motion in thirds or tenths.

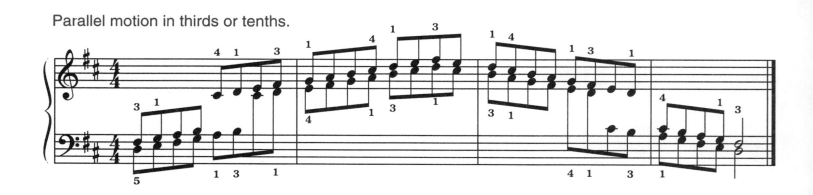

Parallel motion in sixths.

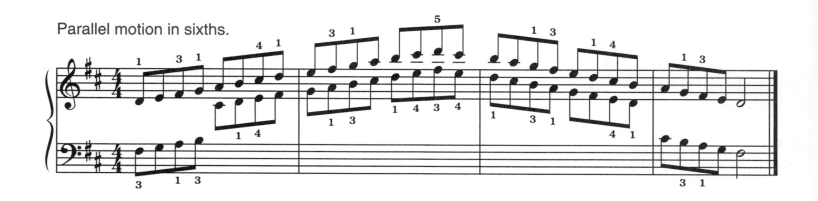

D Major Triads Root position

tonic supertonic mediant subdominant dominant submediant leading tone tonic

D Major Cadences Three Positions

D Major Arpeggios Two-octave arpeggios

Dominant Seventh Arpeggios Two-octave arpeggios

Key of A Major
Major Scales

LH: 4th finger on B (2nd degree).   **RH:** 4th finger on G♯ (7th degree).

Parallel motion in octaves.

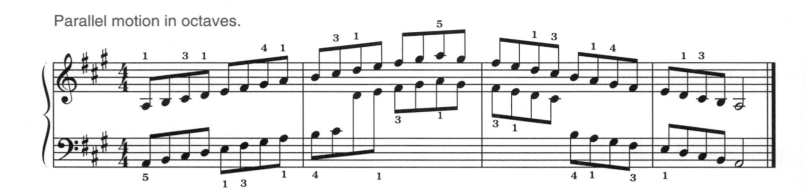

Contrary motion starting on the same note.

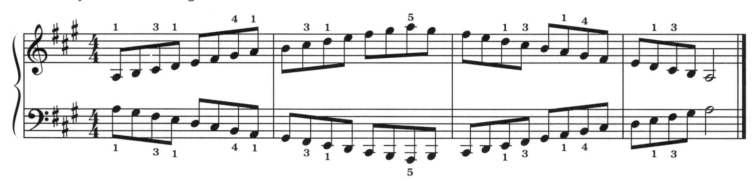

Parallel motion in thirds or tenths.

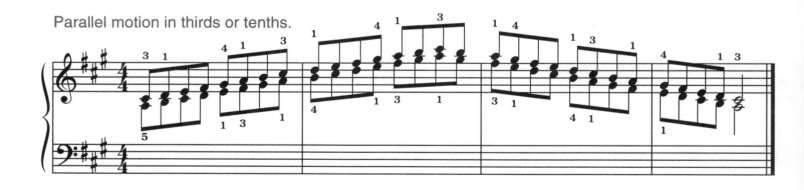

Parallel motion in sixths.

A Major Triads Root position

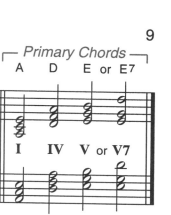

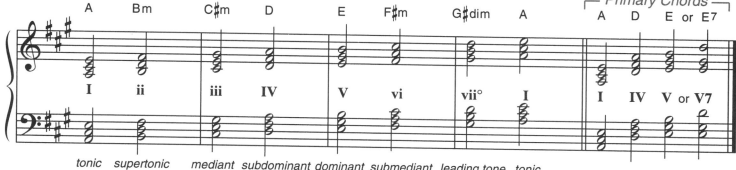

tonic   supertonic   mediant   subdominant   dominant   submediant   leading tone   tonic

A Major Cadences Three Positions

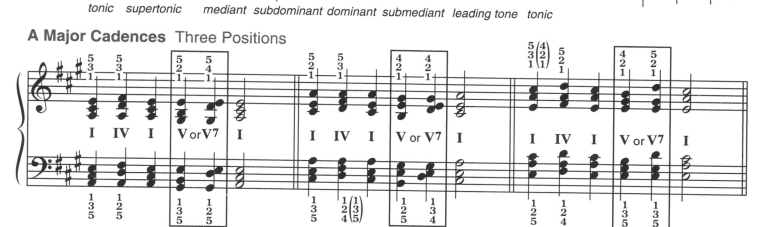

A Major Arpeggios Two-octave arpeggios

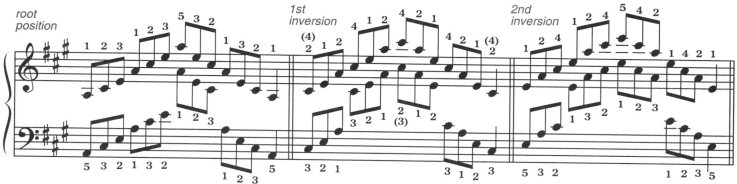

Dominant Seventh Arpeggios Two-octave arpeggios

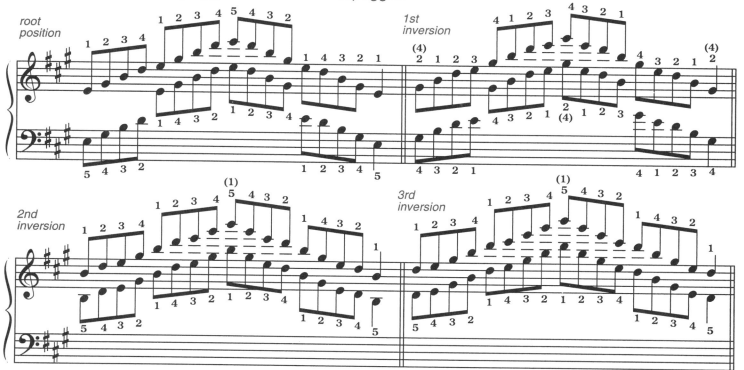

Key of E Major
Major Scales

LH: 4th finger on F♯ (2nd degree). **RH:** 4th finger on D♯ (7th degree).

Parallel motion in octaves.

Contrary motion starting on the same note.

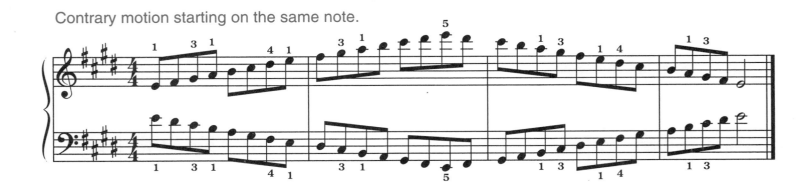

Parallel motion in thirds or tenths.

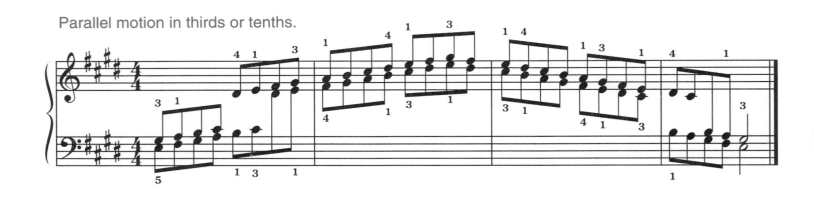

Parallel motion in sixths.

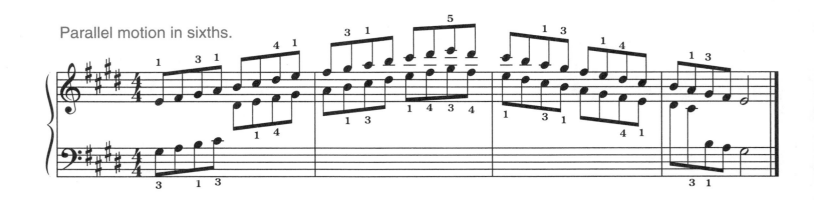

E Major Triads Root position

tonic   supertonic   mediant   subdominant   dominant   submediant   leading tone   tonic

E Major Cadences Three Positions

E Major Arpeggios Two-octave arpeggios

Dominant Seventh Arpeggios Two-octave arpeggios

Key of B Major*

Major Scales

LH: 4th finger on B and F♯ (1st and 5th degrees).** **RH:** 4th finger on A♯ (7th degree).

Parallel motion in octaves.

Contrary motion starting on the same note.

Parallel motion in thirds or tenths.

Parallel motion in sixths.

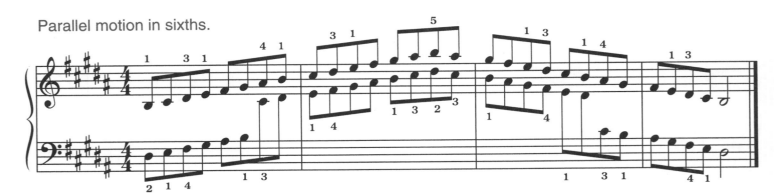

*Enharmonic with C♭ major. See page 30.
**In the 1st octave, LH 4 is used on B—LH 1 thereafter.

13

B Major Triads Root position

B Major Cadences Three Positions

B Major Arpeggios Two-octave arpeggios

Dominant Seventh Arpeggios Two-octave arpeggios

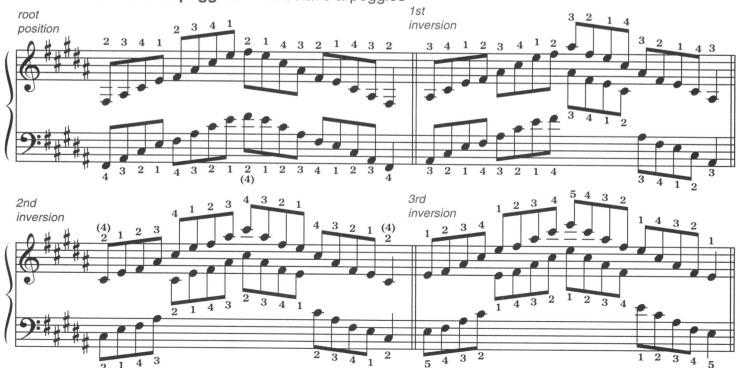

Key of F♯ Major*
Major Scales

LH: 4th finger on F♯ (1st degree).   **RH:** 4th finger on A♯ (3rd degree).

Parallel motion in octaves.

Contrary motion starting on the same note.

Parallel motion in thirds or tenths.

Parallel motion in sixths.

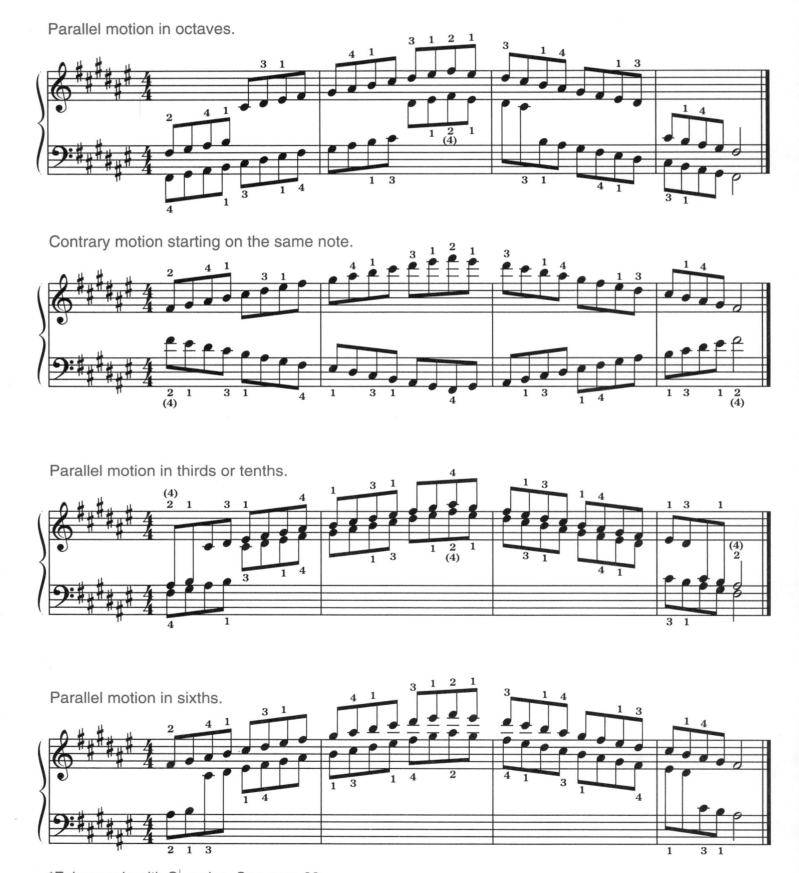

*Enharmonic with G♭ major. See page 28.

F♯ Major Triads Root position

F♯   G♯m   A♯m   B   C♯   D♯m   E♯dim   F♯

┌ *Primary Chords* ┐
F♯   B   C♯ or C♯7

I   ii   iii   IV   V   vi   vii°   I   I   IV   V or V7

tonic supertonic mediant subdomimant dominant submediant leading tone tonic

F♯ Major Cadences Three Positions

I   IV   I   V or V7   I   I   IV   I   V or V7   I   I   IV   I   V or V7   I

F♯ Major Arpeggios Two-octave arpeggios

root position

1st inversion

2nd inversion

Dominant Seventh Arpeggios Two-octave arpeggios

root position

1st inversion

2nd inversion

3rd inversion

Key of C# Major*

Major Scales

LH: 4th finger on F# (4th degree). **RH:** 4th finger on A# (6th degree).

Parallel motion in octaves.

Contrary motion starting on the same note.

Parallel motion in thirds or tenths.

Parallel motion in sixths.

*Enharmonic with Db major. See page 26.

C♯ Major Triads Root position

Primary Chords

C♯ D♯m E♯m F♯ G♯ A♯m B♯dim C♯ C♯ F♯ G♯ or G♯7

I ii iii IV V vi vii° I I IV V or V7

tonic   supertonic   mediant   subdominant   dominant   submediant   leading tone   tonic

C♯ Major Cadences Three Positions

I IV I V or V7 I   I IV I V or V7 I   I IV I V or V7 I

C♯ Major Arpeggios Two-octave arpeggios

root position   1st inversion   2nd inversion

Dominant Seventh Arpeggios Two-octave arpeggios

root position   1st inversion

2nd inversion   3rd inversion

Part 2

Key of F Major
Major Scales

LH: 4th finger on G (2nd degree of scale). **RH:** 4th finger on B♭ (4th degree of scale).

Parallel motion in octaves.

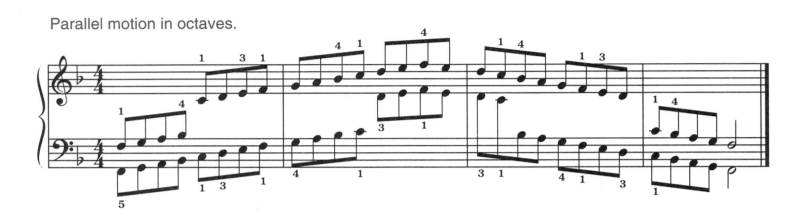

Contrary motion starting on the same note.

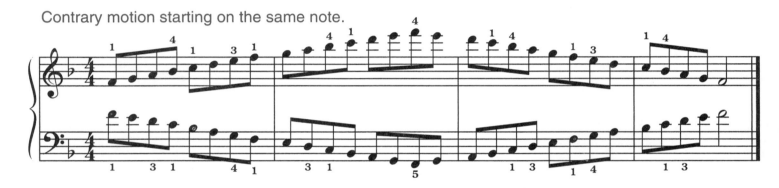

Parallel motion in thirds or tenths.

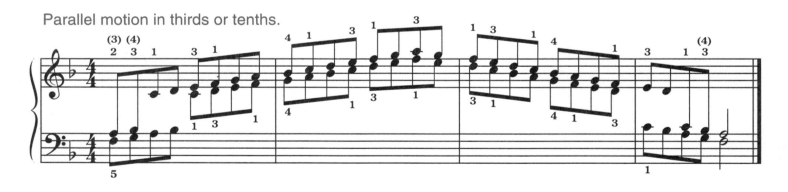

Parallel motion in sixths.

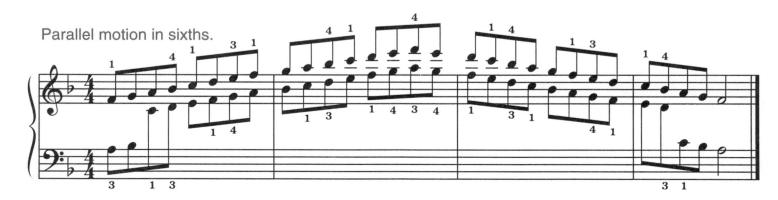

F Major Triads Root position

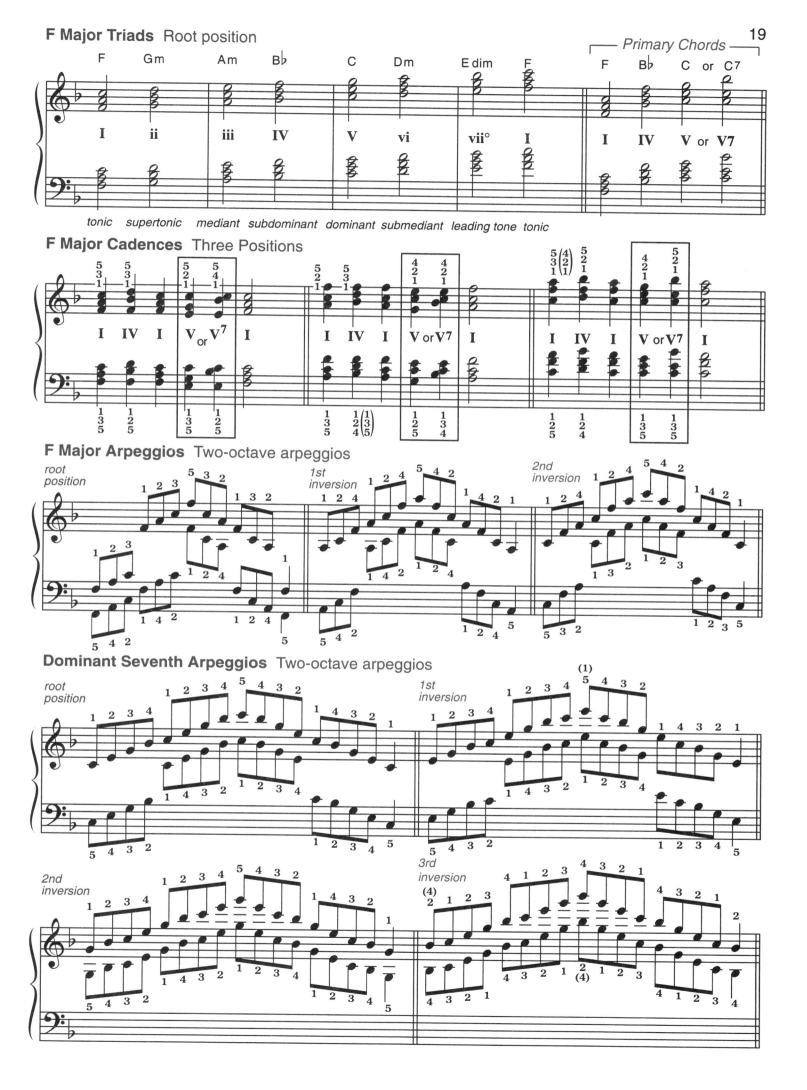

tonic   supertonic   mediant   subdominant   dominant   submediant   leading tone   tonic

F Major Cadences Three Positions

F Major Arpeggios Two-octave arpeggios

Dominant Seventh Arpeggios Two-octave arpeggios

Key of B♭ Major
Major Scales

LH: 4th finger on E♭ (4th degree).   **RH:** 4th finger on B♭ (1st degree).*

Parallel motion in octaves.

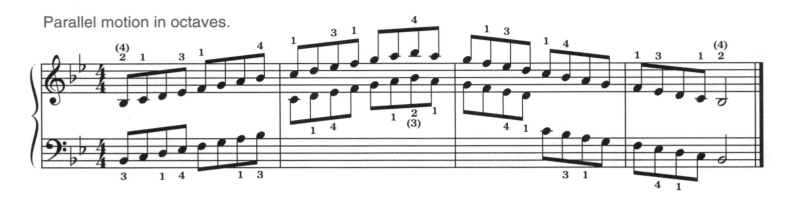

Contrary motion starting on the same note.

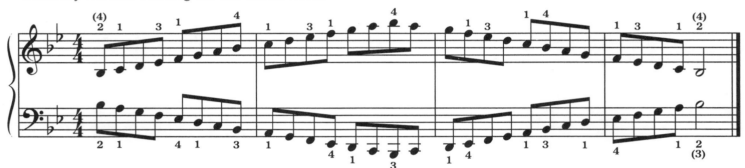

Parallel motion in thirds or tenths.

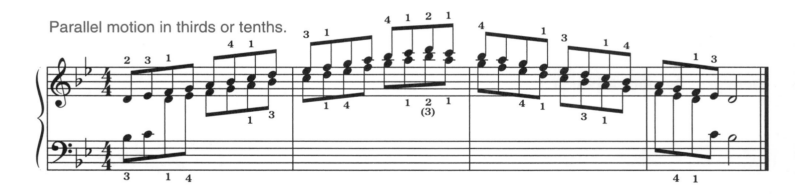

Parallel motion in sixths.

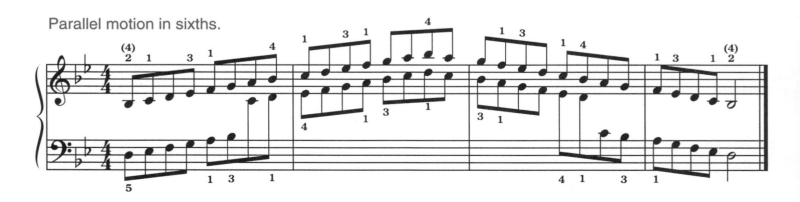

*In the 1st octave, RH 2 or 4 may be used on B♭—RH 4 thereafter.

B♭ Major Triads Root position

Key of E♭ Major
Major Scales

LH: 4th finger on A♭ (4th degree). **RH:** 4th finger on B♭ (5th degree).

Parallel motion in octaves.

Contrary motion starting on the same note.

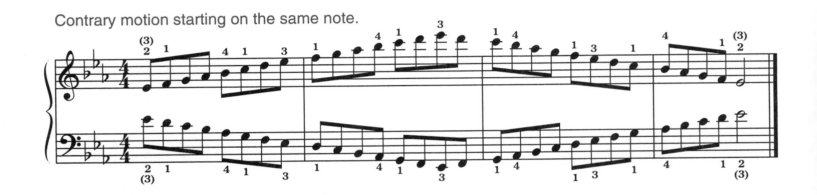

Parallel motion in thirds or tenths.

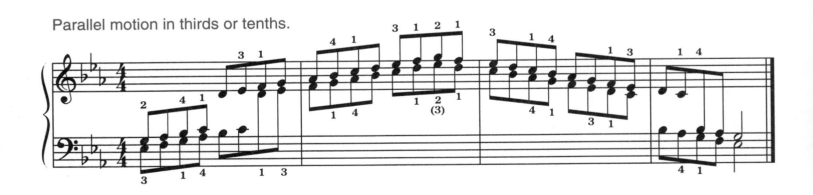

Parallel motion in sixths.

E♭ Major Triads Root position

E♭ Major Cadences Three Positions

E♭ Major Arpeggios Two-octave arpeggios

Dominant Seventh Arpeggios Two-octave arpeggios

Key of A♭ Major
Major Scales

LH: 4th finger on D♭ (4th degree). **RH:** 4th finger on B♭ (2nd degree).*

Parallel motion in octaves.

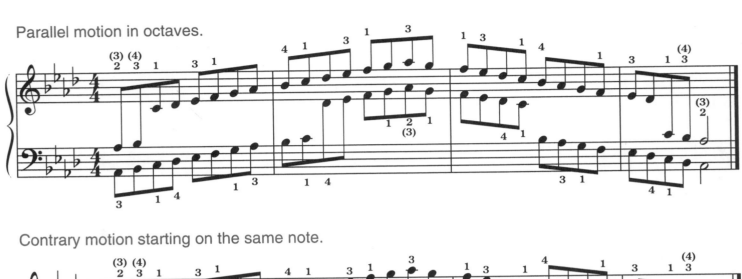

Contrary motion starting on the same note.

Parallel motion in thirds or tenths.

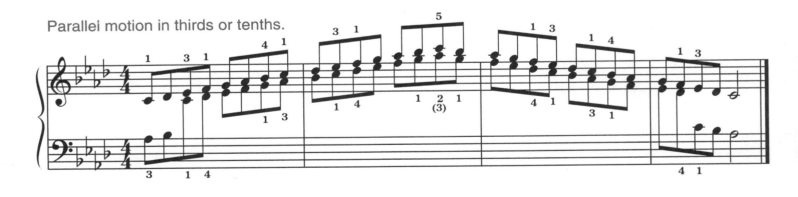

Parallel motion in sixths.

*In the 1st octave, RH 3 or 4 may be used on B♭—RH 4 thereafter.

A♭ Major Triads Root position

tonic supertonic mediant subdominant dominant submediant leading tone tonic

A♭ Major Cadences Three Positions

A♭ Major Arpeggios Two-octave arpeggios

Dominant Seventh Arpeggios Two-octave arpeggios

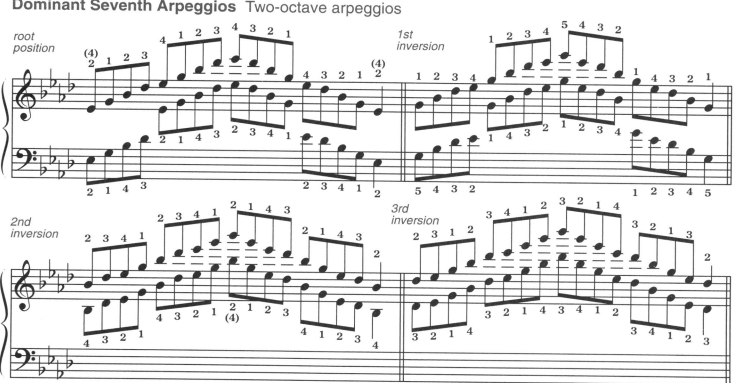

Key of D♭ Major*

Major Scales

LH: 4th finger on G♭ (4th degree). **RH:** 4th finger on B♭ (6th degree).

Parallel motion in octaves.

Contrary motion starting on the same note.

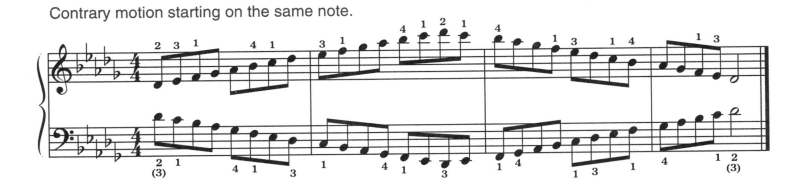

Parallel motion in thirds or tenths.

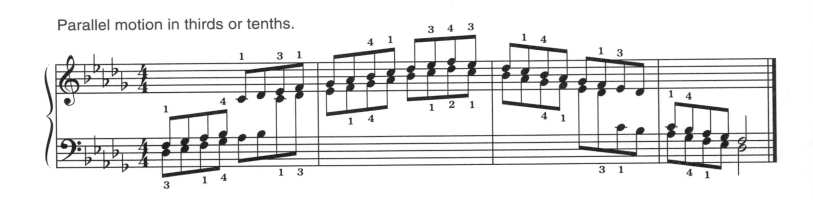

Parallel motion in sixths.

*Enharmonic with C♯ major. See page 16.

Db Major Triads Root position

Primary Chords

Db Major Cadences Three Positions

Db Major Arpeggios Two-octave arpeggios

Dominant Seventh Arpeggios Two-octave arpeggios

Key of G♭ Major*

Major Scales

LH: 4th finger on G♭ (1st degree). **RH:** 4th finger on B♭ (3rd degree).

Parallel motion in octaves.

Contrary motion starting on the same note.

Parallel motion in thirds or tenths.

Parallel motion in sixths.

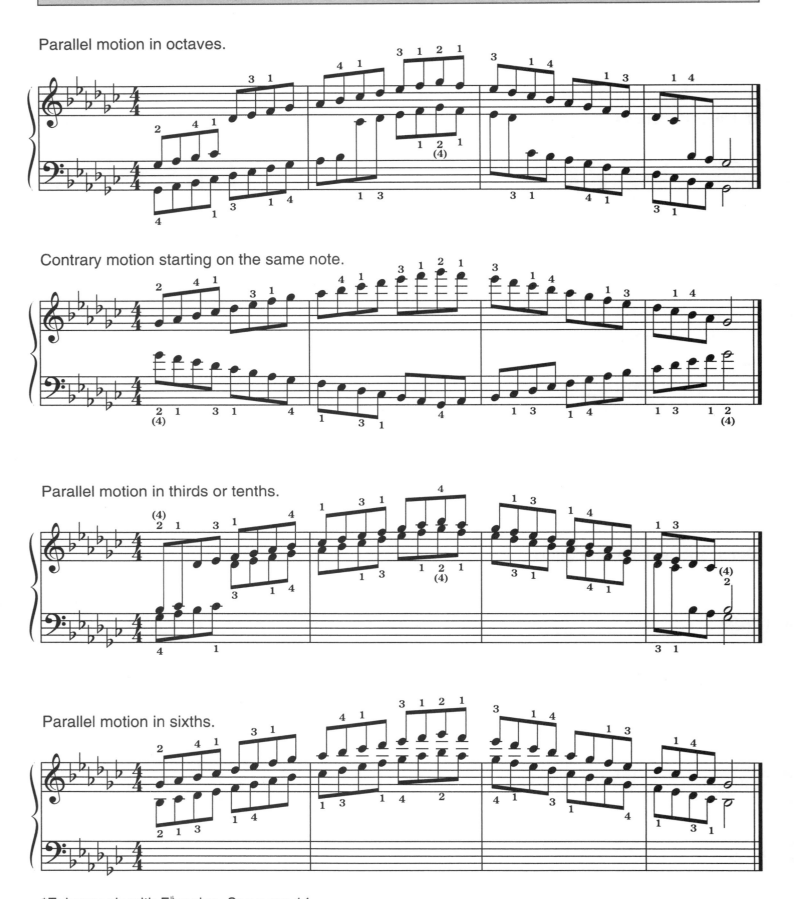

*Enharmonic with F♯ major. See page 14.

G♭ Major Triads Root position

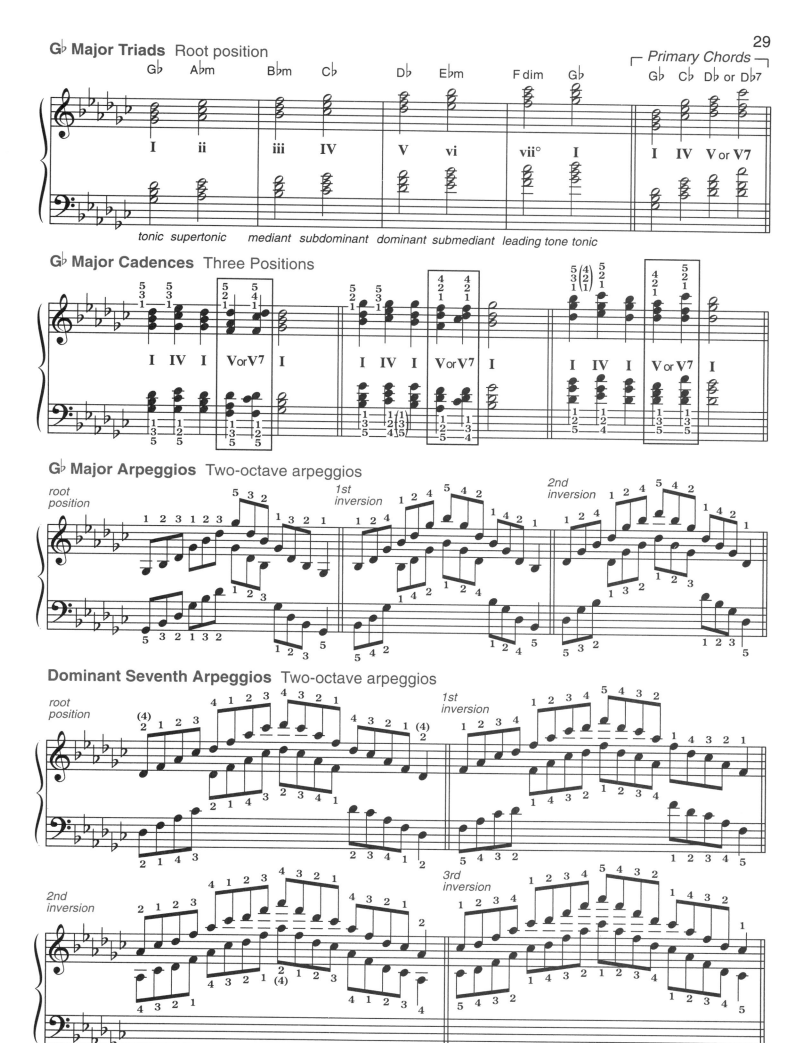

G♭   A♭m   B♭m   C♭   D♭   E♭m   F dim   G♭

I   ii   iii   IV   V   vi   vii°   I

Primary Chords
G♭   C♭   D♭ or D♭7

I   IV   V or V7

tonic supertonic   mediant subdominant dominant submediant leading tone tonic

G♭ Major Cadences Three Positions

I   IV   I   V or V7   I   I   IV   I   V or V7   I   I   IV   I   V or V7   I

G♭ Major Arpeggios Two-octave arpeggios

root position   1st inversion   2nd inversion

Dominant Seventh Arpeggios Two-octave arpeggios

root position   1st inversion

2nd inversion   3rd inversion

Key of C♭ Major*

Major Scales

LH: 4th finger on C♭ and G♭ (1st and 5th degrees).** **RH:** 4th finger on B♭ (7th degree).

Parallel motion in octaves.

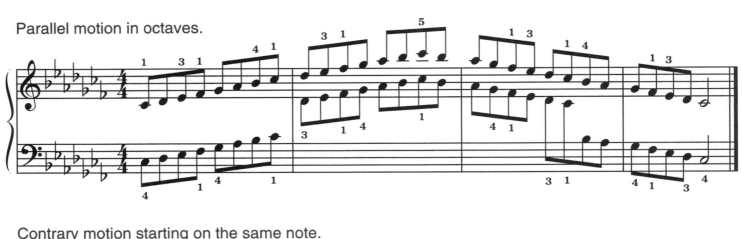

Contrary motion starting on the same note.

Parallel motion in thirds or tenths.

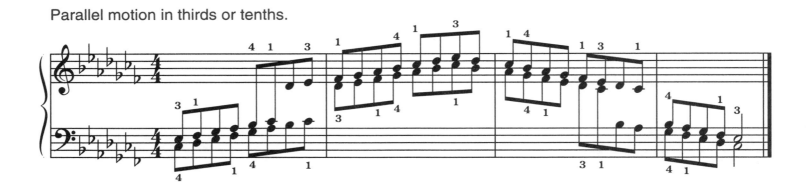

Parallel motion in sixths.

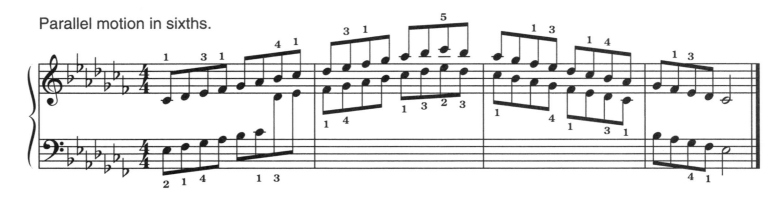

*Enharmonic with B major. See page 12.
**In the 1st octave, LH 4 is used on C♭—LH 1 thereafter.

C♭ Major Triads Root position

tonic supertonic mediant subdominant dominant submediant leading tone tonic

C♭ Major Cadences Three Positions

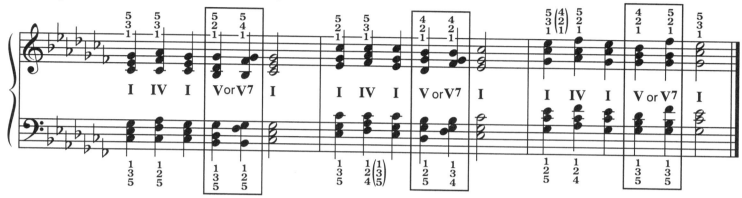

C♭ Major Arpeggios Two-octave arpeggios

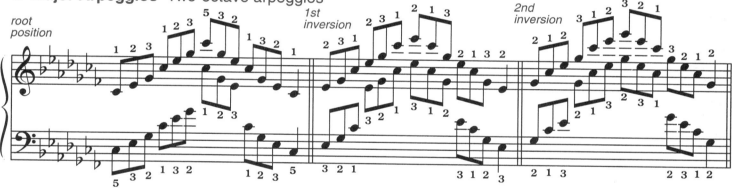

Dominant Seventh Arpeggios Two-octave arpeggios

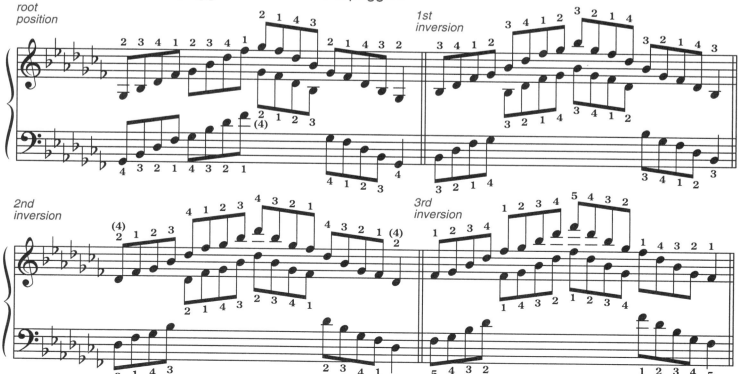

Key of A Minor

Part 3

Relative Minor of C Major

LH: 4th finger on B (2nd degree of scale).   **RH:** 4th finger on G or G♯ (7th degree of scale).

Natural minor scale, parallel motion in octaves.

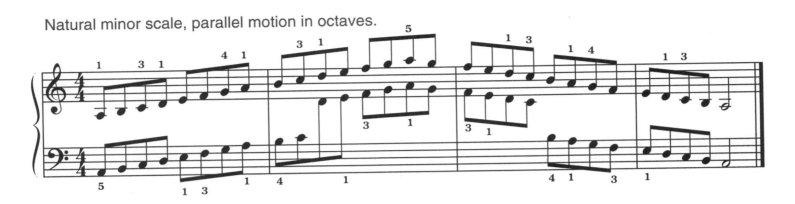

Harmonic minor scale, parallel motion in octaves.

Harmonic minor scale, contrary motion.

Melodic minor scale, parallel motion in octaves. RH 4th finger on G♯ ascending, G♮ descending.

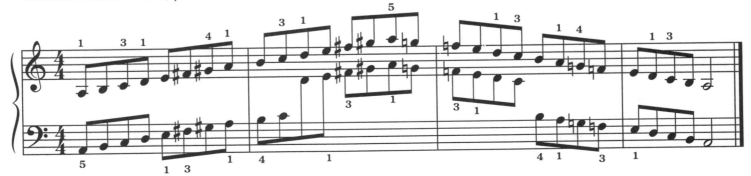

A Minor Triads Root position

Am B dim C aug Dm E F G♯dim Am

Primary Chords

Am Dm E or E7

i ii° III⁺ iv V VI vii° i i iv V or V7

tonic supertonic mediant subdominant dominant submediant leading tone tonic

A Minor Cadences Three positions

i iv i V or V7 i i iv i V or V7 i i iv i V or V7 i

A Minor Arpeggios Two-octave arpeggios, three positions

root position 1st inversion 2nd inversion

Diminished Seventh Arpeggios Two-octave arpeggios, four positions

root position 1st inversion

2nd inversion 3rd inversion

Key of E Minor
Relative Minor of G Major

LH: 4th finger on F# (2nd degree).   **RH:** 4th finger on D or D# (7th degree).

Natural minor scale, parallel motion in octaves.

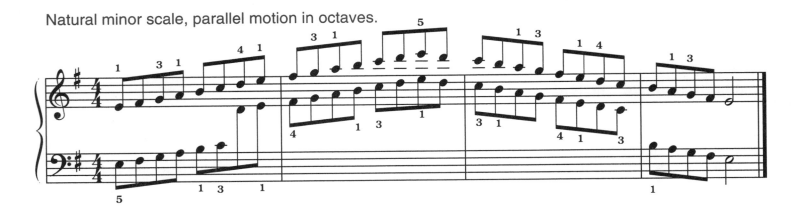

Harmonic minor scale, parallel motion in octaves.

Harmonic minor scale, contrary motion.

Melodic minor scale, parallel motion in octaves. RH 4th finger on D# ascending, D♮ descending.

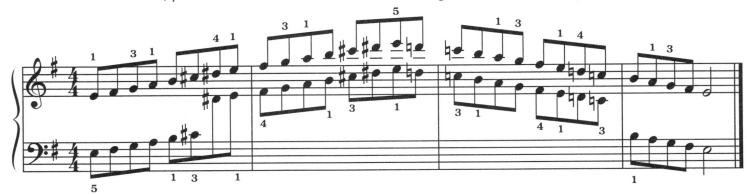

E Minor Triads Root position

Key of B Minor
Relative Minor of D Major

LH: 4th finger on B and F♯ (1st and 5th degrees).*   **RH:** 4th finger on A or A♯ (7th degree).

Natural minor scale, parallel motion in octaves.

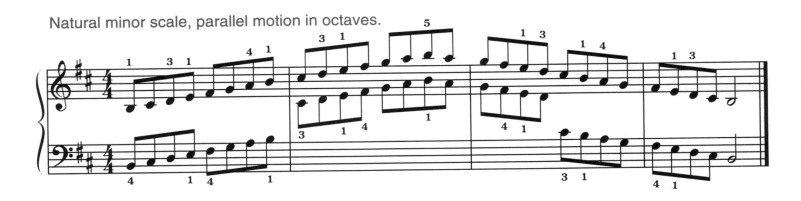

Harmonic minor scale, parallel motion in octaves.

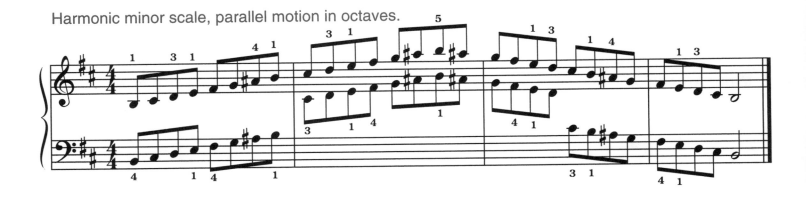

Harmonic minor scale, contrary motion.

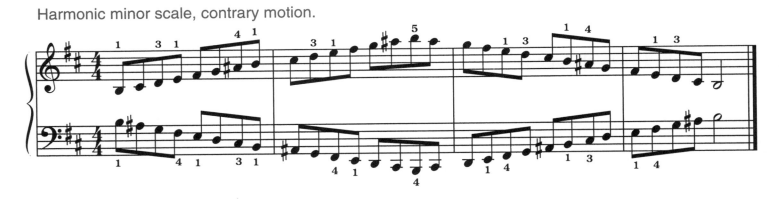

Melodic minor scale, parallel motion in octaves. RH 4th finger on A♯ ascending, A♮ descending.

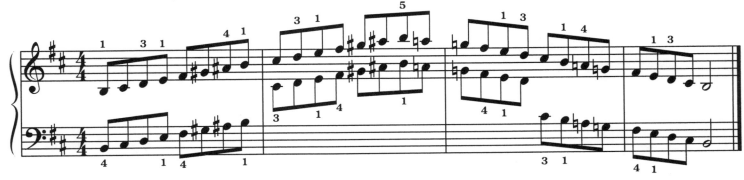

*In the 1st octave, LH 4 is used on B—LH 1 thereafter.

B Minor Triads Root position

B Minor Cadences Three positions

B Minor Arpeggios Two-octave arpeggios, three positions

A♯ Diminished Seventh Arpeggios Two-octave arpeggios, four positions

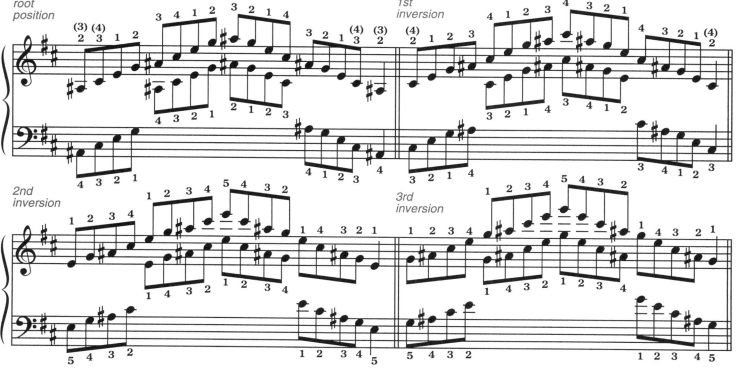

Key of F♯ Minor
Relative Minor of A Major

LH: 4th finger on F♯ (1st degree). **RH:** 4th finger on G♯ (2nd degree).*

Natural minor scale, parallel motion in octaves.

Harmonic minor scale, parallel motion in octaves.

Harmonic minor scale, contrary motion.

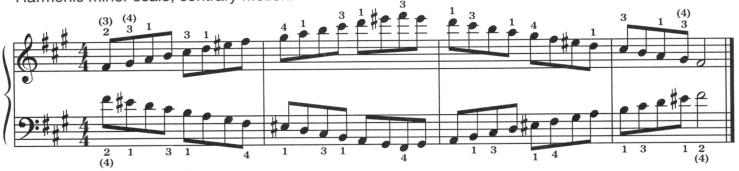

Melodic minor scale, parallel motion in octaves. RH 4th finger on D♯ ascending, G♯ descending.

*In the 1st octave, RH 3 or 4 may be used on G♯—RH 4 thereafter.

F♯ Minor Triads Root position

Primary Chords

F♯m	G♯dim	Aaug	Bm	C♯	D	E♯dim	F♯m	F♯m	Bm	C♯ or C♯7
i	ii°	III+	iv	V	VI	vii°	i	i	iv	V or V7

tonic   supertonic   mediant   subdominant   dominant   submediant   leading tone   tonic

F♯ Minor Cadences Three positions

i   iv   i   V or V7   i   i   iv   i   V or V7   i   i   iv   i   V or V7   i

F♯ Minor Arpeggios Two-octave arpeggios, three positions

root position   1st inversion   2nd inversion

E♯ Diminished Seventh Arpeggios Two-octave arpeggios, four positions

root position   1st inversion

2nd inversion   Both hands 8va - - - -   3rd inversion   Both hands 8va - - - -

40

Key of C# Minor
Relative Minor of E Major

LH: 4th finger on F# (4th degree).   **RH:** 4th finger on D# (2nd degree).*

Natural minor scale, parallel motion in octaves.

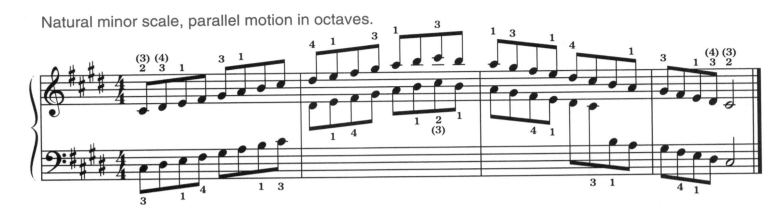

Harmonic minor scale, parallel motion in octaves.

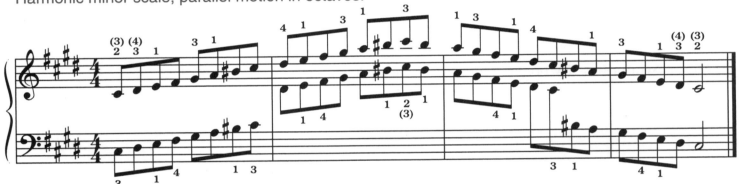

Harmonic minor scale, contrary motion.

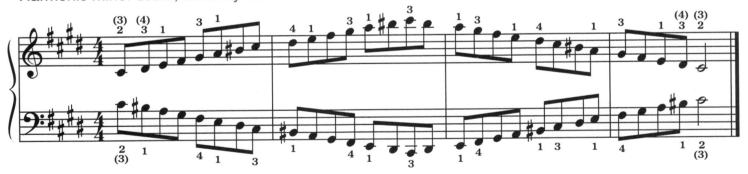

Melodic minor scale, parallel motion in octaves. RH 4th finger on A# ascending, D# descending.

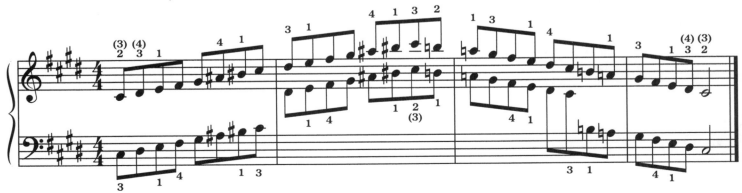

*In the 1st octave, RH 3 or 4 may be used on D#—RH 4 thereafter.

C♯ Minor Triads Root position

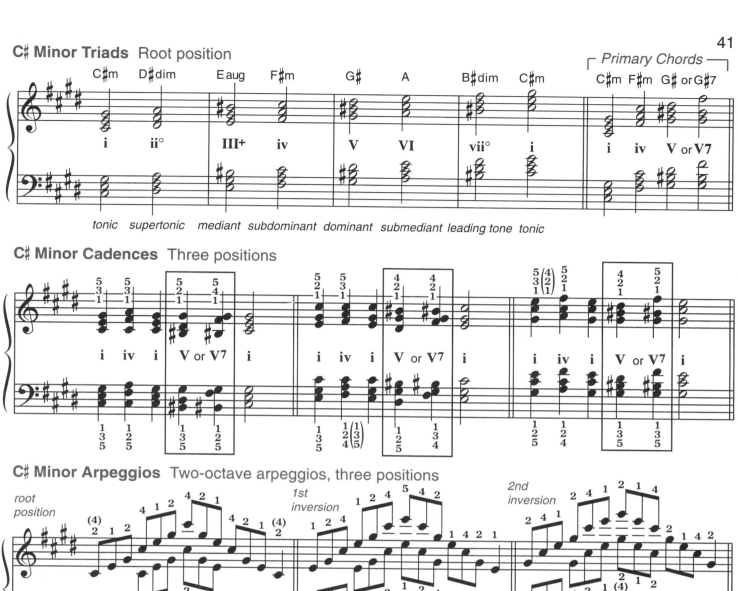

C♯m · D♯dim · E aug · F♯m · G♯ · A · B♯dim · C♯m · *Primary Chords* C♯m F♯m G♯ or G♯7

i · ii° · III+ · iv · V · VI · vii° · i · i iv V or V7

tonic · supertonic · mediant · subdominant · dominant · submediant · leading tone · tonic

C♯ Minor Cadences Three positions

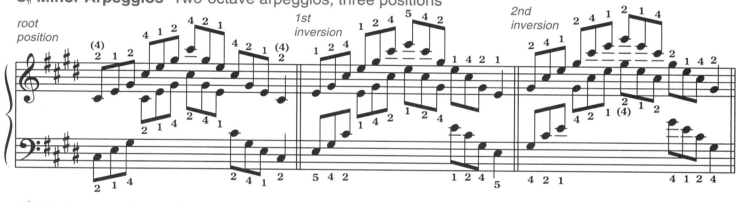

i iv i V or V7 i · i iv i V or V7 i · i iv i V or V7 i

C♯ Minor Arpeggios Two-octave arpeggios, three positions

B♯ Diminished Seventh Arpeggios Two-octave arpeggios, four positions

Key of G♯ Minor*
Relative Minor of B Major

LH: 4th finger on C♯ (4th degree).   **RH:** 4th finger on A♯ (2nd degree).**

Natural minor scale, parallel motion in octaves. LH 4th finger on F♯ (7th degree).

This is the only scale where the LH fingering in the *natural* minor differs from the *harmonic* minor.

Harmonic minor scale, parallel motion in octaves.

Harmonic minor scale, contrary motion.

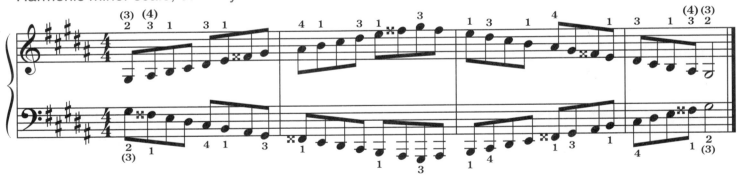

Melodic minor scale, parallel motion in octaves. LH 4th finger on C♯ ascending, F♯ descending.

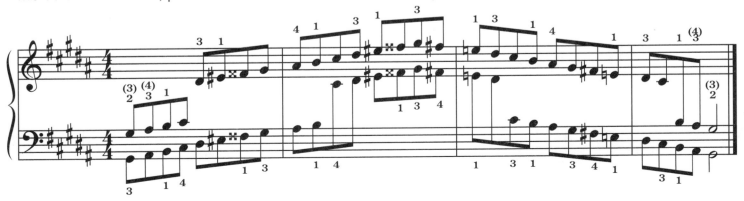

*Enharmonic with A♭ minor. See page 60.
**In the 1st octave, RH 3 or 4 may be used on A♯—RH 4 thereafter.

G# Minor Triads Root position

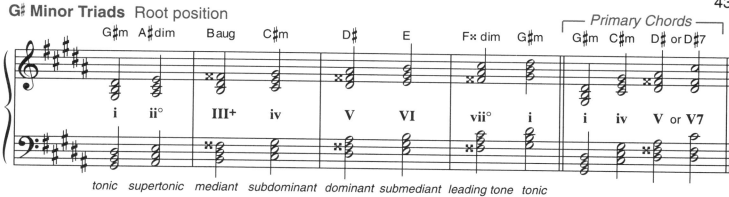

G# Minor Cadences Three positions

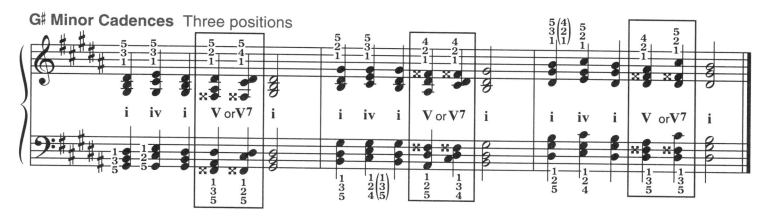

G# Minor Arpeggios Two-octave arpeggios, three positions

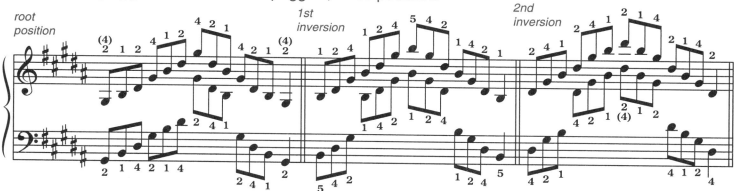

Fx Diminished Seventh Arpeggios Two-octave arpeggios, four positions

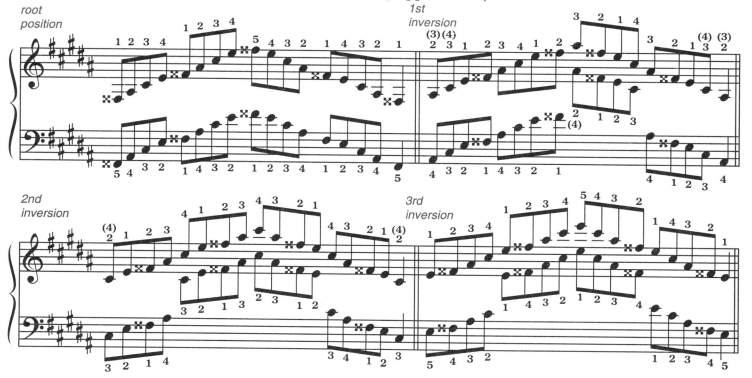

Key of D♯ Minor*
Relative Minor of F♯ Major

LH: 4th finger on F♯ (3rd degree).   **RH:** 4th finger on A♯ (5th degree).

Natural minor scale, parallel motion in octaves.

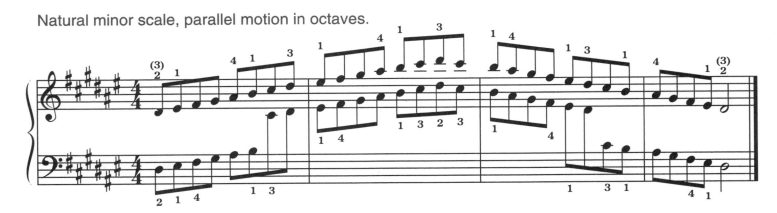

Harmonic minor scale, parallel motion in octaves.

Harmonic minor scale, contrary motion.

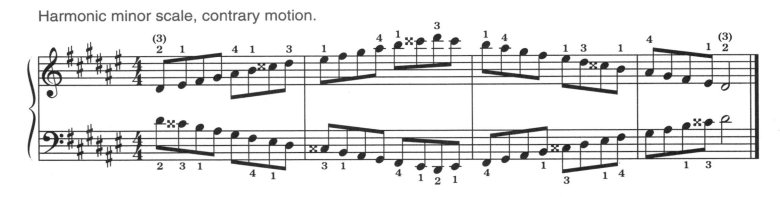

Melodic minor scale, parallel motion in octaves.

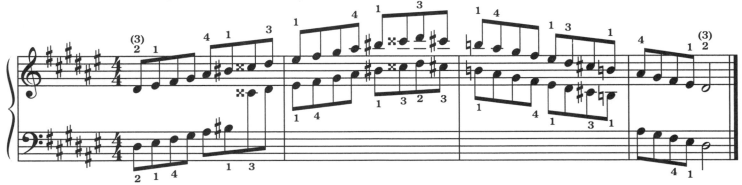

*Enharmonic with E♭ minor. See page 58.

Key of A♯ Minor*
Relative Minor of C♯ Major

LH: 4th finger on F♯ or F𝄪 (6th degree).   **RH:** 4th finger on A♯ (1st degree).**

Natural minor scale, parallel motion in octaves.

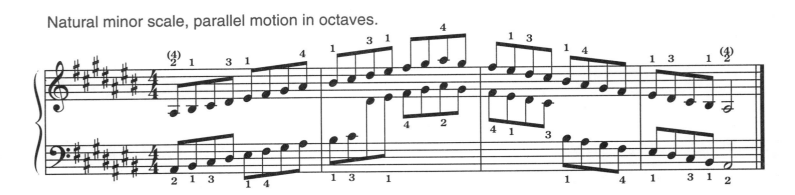

Harmonic minor scale, parallel motion in octaves.

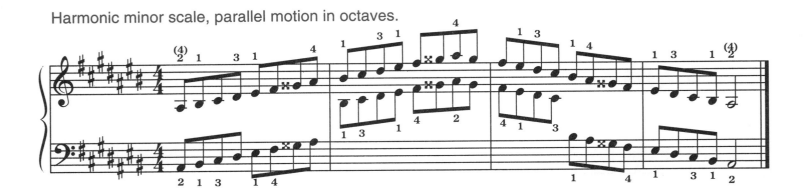

Harmonic minor scale, contrary motion.

Melodic minor scale, parallel motion in octaves. LH 4 on F𝄪 ascending, F♯ descending.

*Enharmonic with B♭ minor. See page 56.
**In the 1st octave, RH 2 or 4 may be used on the A♯—RH 4 thereafter.

A# Minor Triads Root position

A#m B#dim   C#aug D#m   E#   F#   G×dim A#m   A#m D#m E# or E#7

i   ii°   III+   iv   V   VI   vii°   i   i   iv   V or V7

tonic   supertonic   mediant   subdominant   dominant   submediant   leading tone   tonic

A# Minor Cadences Three positions

i iv i V or V7 i   i iv i V or V7 i   i iv i V or V7 i

A# Minor Arpeggios Two-octave arpeggios, three positions

root position   1st inversion   2nd inversion

G× Diminished Seventh Arpeggios Two-octave arpeggios, four positions

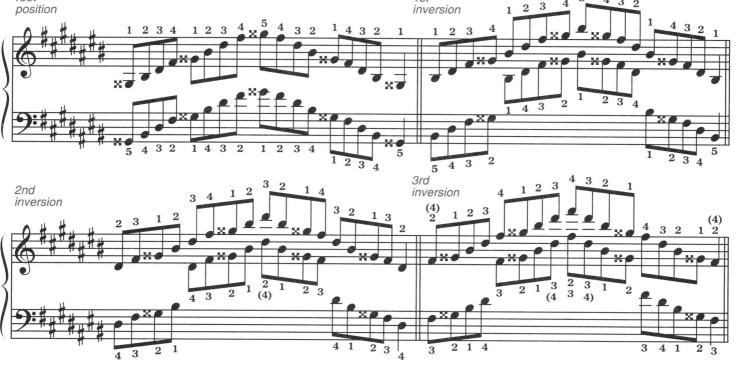

root position   1st inversion

2nd inversion   3rd inversion

Part 4

Key of D Minor
Relative Minor of F Major

LH: 4th finger on E (2nd degree of scale).   **RH:** 4th finger on C or C♯ (7th degree of scale).

Natural minor scale, parallel motion in octaves.

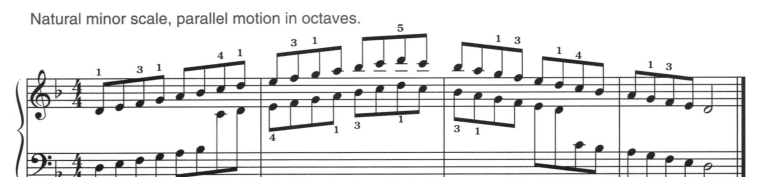

Harmonic minor scale, parallel motion in octaves.

Harmonic minor scale, contrary motion.

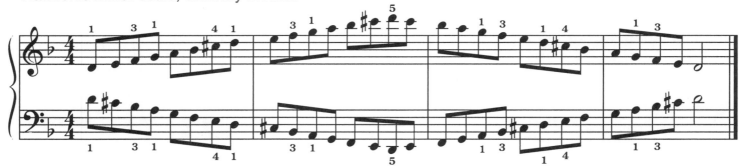

Melodic minor scale, parallel motion in octaves. RH 4th finger on C♯ ascending, C♮ descending.

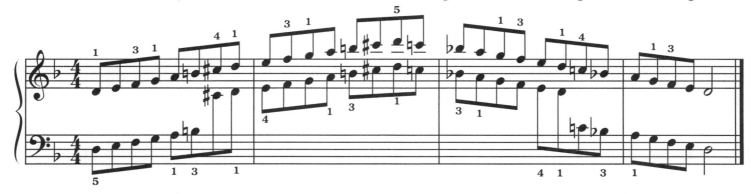

D Minor Triads Root position

Dm E dim F aug Gm A B♭ C♯dim Dm

i ii° III+ iv V VI vii° i

Primary Chords

Dm Gm A or A7

i iv V or V7

tonic supertonic mediant subdominant dominant submediant leading tone tonic

D Minor Cadences Three positions

i iv i V or V7 i

i iv i V or V7 i

i iv i V or V7 i

D Minor Arpeggios Two-octave arpeggios, three positions

root position

Play LH 8va

1st inversion

2nd inversion

C♯ Diminished Seventh Arpeggios Two-octave arpeggios, four positions

root position

1st inversion

2nd inversion

3rd inversion

Key of G Minor

Relative Minor of B♭ Major

LH: 4th finger on A (2nd degree).   **RH:** 4th finger on F or F♯ (7th degree).

Natural minor scale, parallel motion in octaves.

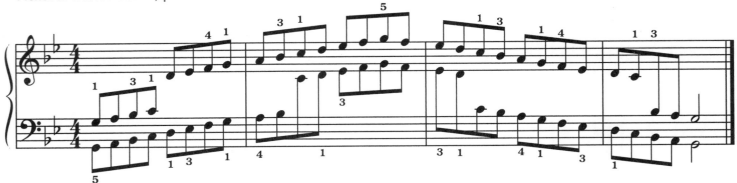

Harmonic minor scale, parallel motion in octaves.

Harmonic minor scale, contrary motion.

Melodic minor scale, parallel motion in octaves. RH 4th finger on F♯ ascending, F♮ descending.

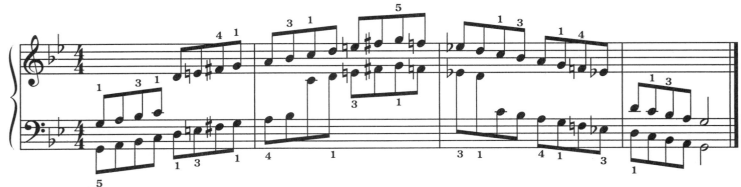

G Minor Triads Root position

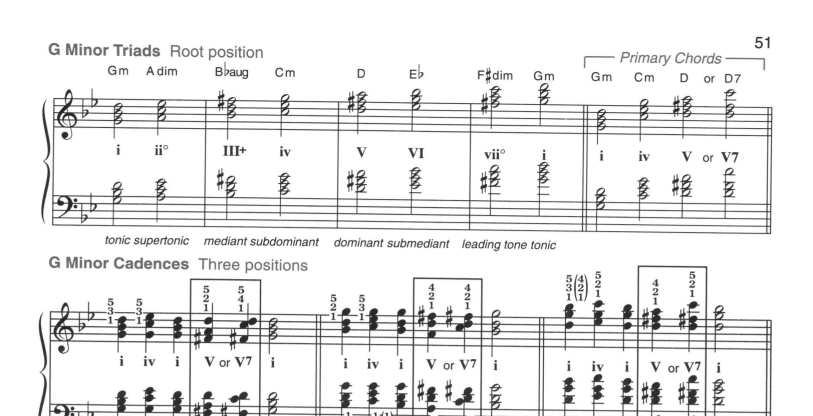

G Minor Cadences Three positions

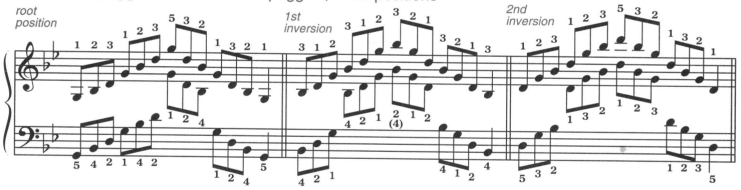

G Minor Arpeggios Two-octave arpeggios, three positions

F# Diminished Seventh Arpeggios Two-octave arpeggios, four positions

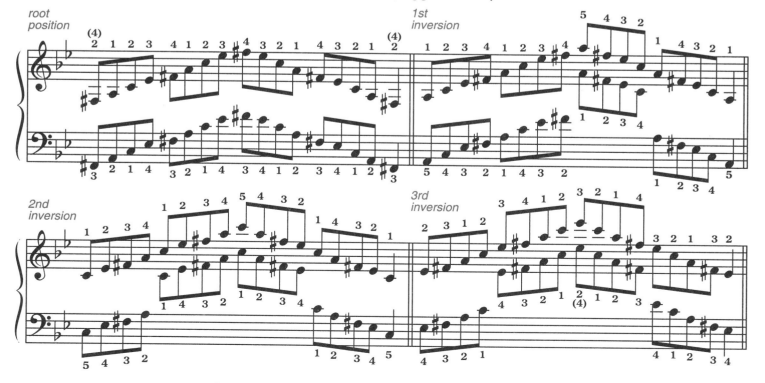

Key of C Minor
Relative Minor of E♭ Major

LH: 4th finger on D (2nd degree).   **RH:** 4th finger on B or B♭ (7th degree).

Natural minor scale, parallel motion in octaves.

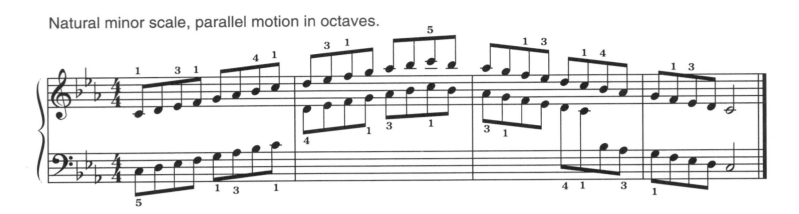

Harmonic minor scale, parallel motion in octaves.

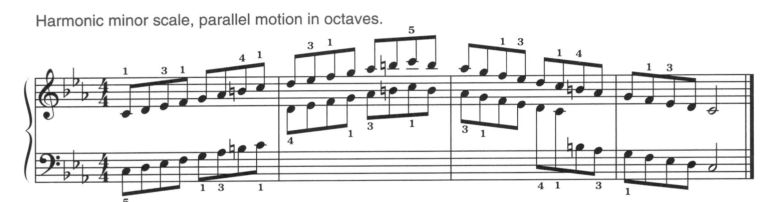

Harmonic minor scale, contrary motion.

Melodic minor scale, parallel motion in octaves. RH 4th finger on B♮ ascending, B♭ descending.

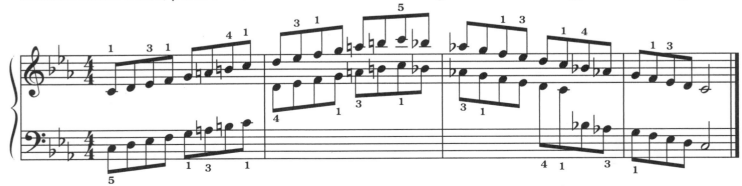

C Minor Triads Root position

Key of F Minor
Relative Minor of A♭ Major

LH: 4th finger on G (2nd degree).   **RH:** 4th finger on B♭ (4th degree).

Natural minor scale, parallel motion in octaves.

Harmonic minor scale, parallel motion in octaves.

Harmonic minor scale, contrary motion.

Melodic minor scale, parallel motion in octaves.

F Minor Triads Root position

Fm	G dim	A♭aug	B♭m	C	D♭	E dim	Fm	Fm	B♭m	C or C7
i	ii°	III+	iv	V	VI	vii°	i	i	iv	V or V7

tonic   supertonic   mediant   subdominant   dominant   submediant   leading tone   tonic

F Minor Cadences Three positions

i   iv   i   V or V7   i   i   iv   i   V or V7   i   i   iv   i   V or V7   i

F Minor Arpeggios Two-octave arpeggios, three positions

root position   *1st inversion*   *2nd inversion*

E Diminished Seventh Arpeggios Two-octave arpeggios, four positions

root position   *1st inversion*

2nd inversion   *3rd inversion*

Key of B♭ Minor*
Relative Minor of D♭ Major

LH: 4th finger on G or G♭ (6th degree).   **RH:** 4th finger on B♭ (1st degree).**

Natural minor scale, parallel motion in octaves.

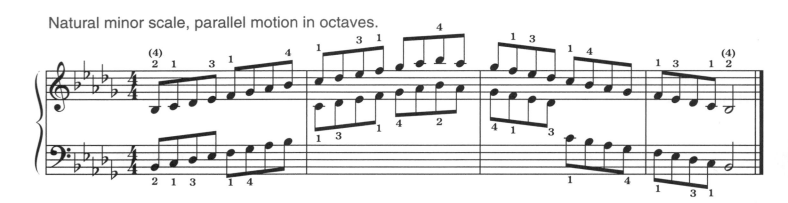

Harmonic minor scale, parallel motion in octaves.

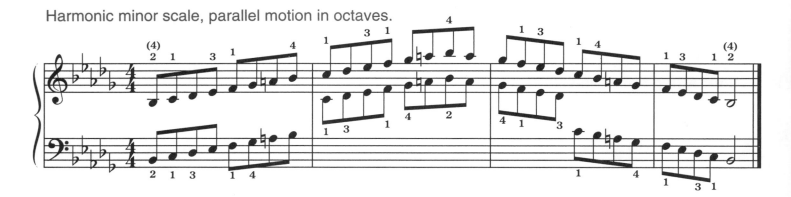

Harmonic minor scale, contrary motion.

Melodic minor scale, parallel motion in octaves. LH 4th finger on G♮ ascending, G♭ descending.

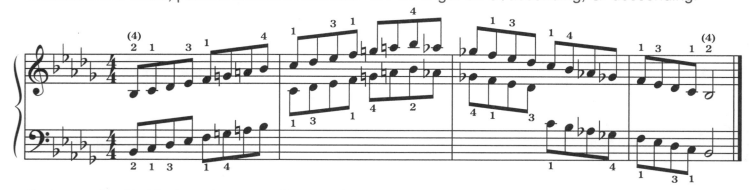

*Enharmonic with A♯ minor. See page 46.
**In the 1st octave, RH 2 or 4 may be used on B♭—RH 4 thereafter.

B♭ Minor Triads Root position

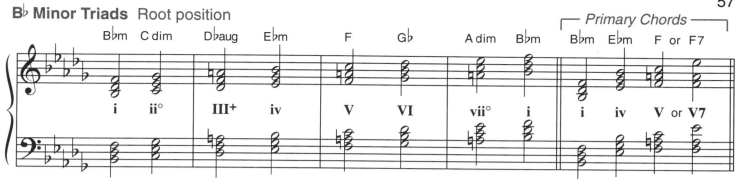

B♭ Minor Cadences Three positions

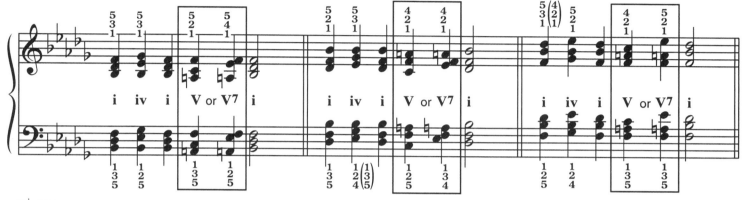

B♭ Minor Arpeggios Two-octave arpeggios, three positions

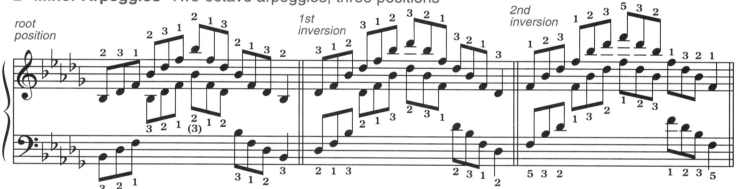

A Diminished Seventh Arpeggios Two-octave arpeggios, four positions

Key of E♭ Minor*
Relative Minor of G♭ Major

LH: 4th finger on G♭ (3rd degree). **RH:** 4th finger on B♭ (5th degree).

Natural minor scale, parallel motion in octaves.

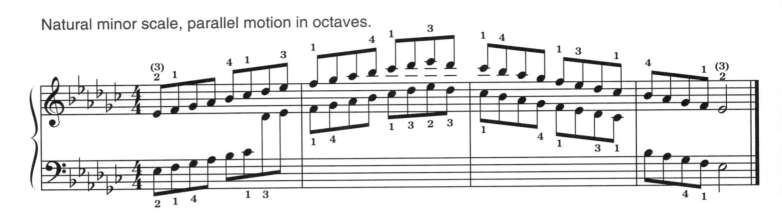

Harmonic minor scale, parallel motion in octaves.

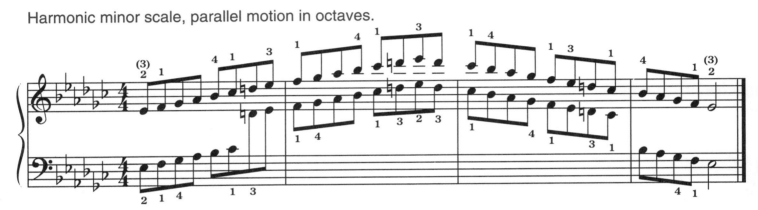

Harmonic minor scale, contrary motion.

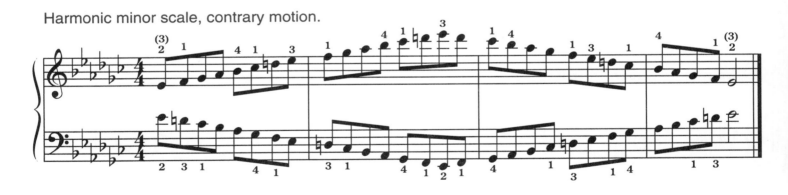

Melodic minor scale, parallel motion in octaves.

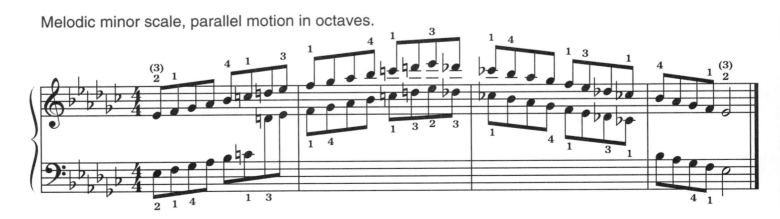

*Enharmonic with D♯ minor. See page 44.

E♭ Minor Triads Root position

tonic supertonic mediant subdominant dominant submediant leading tone tonic

E♭ Minor Cadences Three positions

E♭ Minor Arpeggios Two-octave arpeggios, three positions

D Diminished Seventh Arpeggios Two-octave arpeggios, four positions

Key of A♭ Minor*

Relative Minor of C♭ Major

LH: 4th finger on D♭ (4th degree). **RH:** 4th finger on B♭ (2nd degree).**

Natural minor scale, parallel motion in octaves. LH 4th finger on G♭ (7th degree).

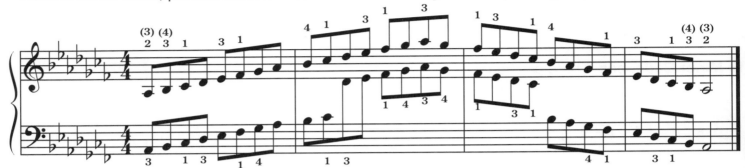

This is the only scale where the LH fingering in the *natural* minor differs from the *harmonic* minor.

Harmonic minor scale, parallel motion in octaves.

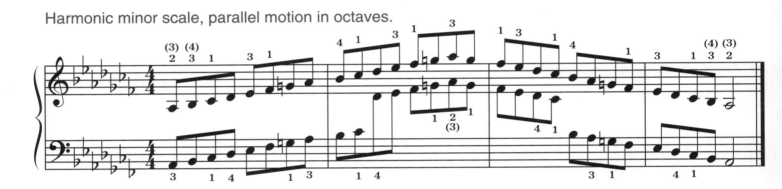

Harmonic minor scale, contrary motion.

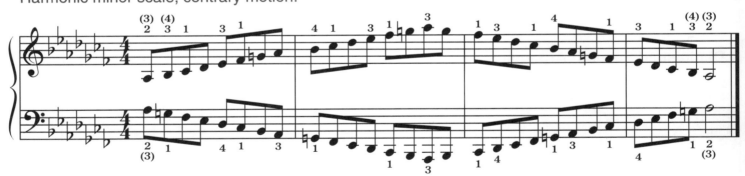

Melodic minor scale, parallel motion in octaves. LH 4th finger on D♭ ascending, G♭ descending.

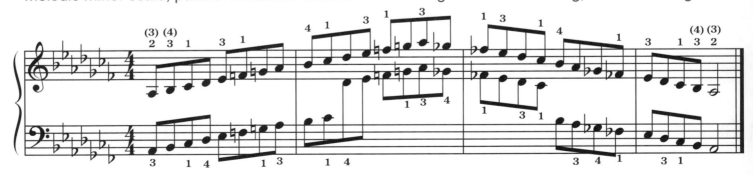

*Enharmonic with G♯ minor. See page 42.
**In the 1st octave, RH 3 or 4 may be used on B♭—RH 4 thereafter.

A♭ Minor Triads Root position

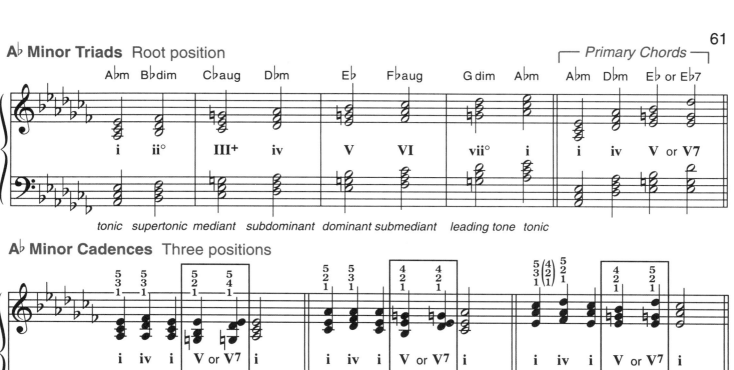

A♭ Minor Cadences Three positions

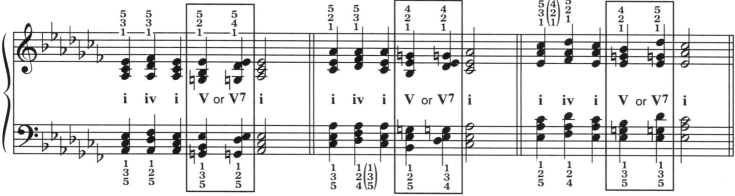

A♭ Minor Arpeggios Two-octave arpeggios, three positions

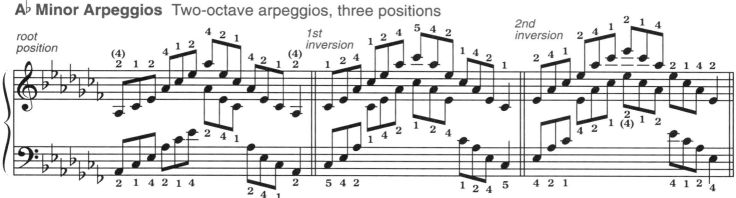

G Diminished Seventh Arpeggios Two-octave arpeggios, four positions

Chromatic Scales
Parallel Motion

Parallel motion in octaves.

Parallel motion in minor thirds or tenths.

Parallel motion in major thirds or tenths.

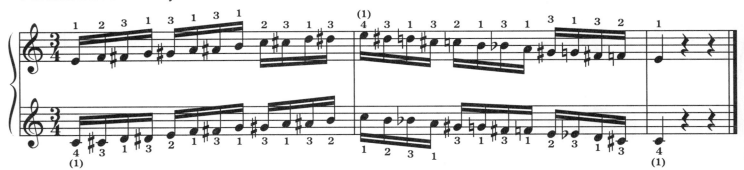

Parallel motion in minor sixths.

Parallel motion in major sixths.

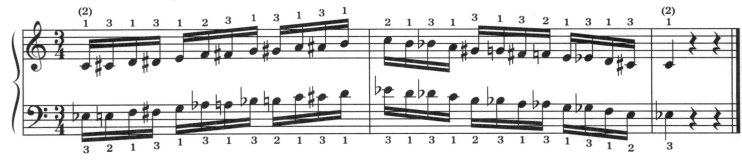

Chromatic Scales
Contrary Motion

Contrary motion beginning in unison.

Contrary motion beginning at minor third or tenth.

Contrary motion at major third or tenth.

Contrary motion beginning at minor sixth.

Contrary motion beginning at major sixth.

Scales in Double Thirds, Double Sixths and Octaves.

C major in double thirds—staccato only

C major in double sixths—staccato only

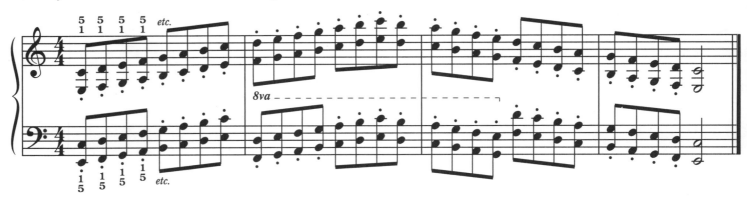

C major in octaves—staccato only (Optional: in scales using black keys, the thumb and 4th finger may be used on the black keys in both hands.)

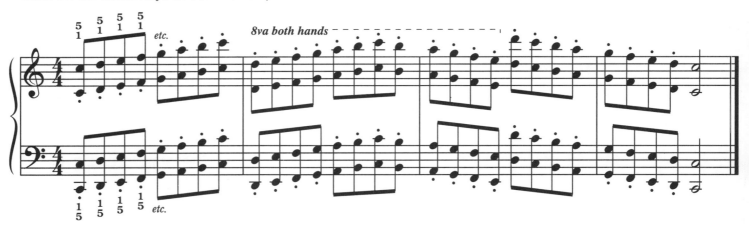

C major in double thirds—legato only.

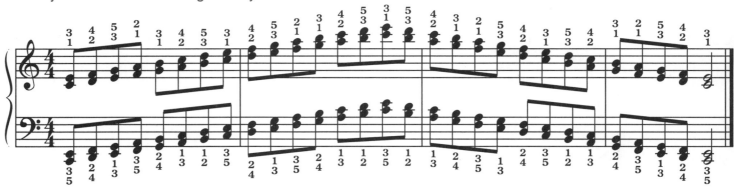